The Power Of Positive Thinking

Keep your thoughts p
thoughts become your words. Keep your
words positive because your words become
your behaviour."

– Mahatma Gandhi

"If you can dream
it, you can do it." –
Walt Disney

Kevin M Gould

Copyright © *Kevin M Gould*, 2025

All Rights Reserved

This book is subject to the condition that no part of this book is to be reproduced, transmitted in any form or means; electronic or mechanical, stored in a retrieval system, photocopied, recorded, scanned, or otherwise. Any of these actions require the proper written permission of the author.

Table of Contents

The Power of Positive Thinking.......................1

A note from the author 3

Chapter 1 Understanding the Mind 8

Chapter 2 Benefits of Positive Thinking 13

Chapter 3 Identifying Negative Patterns: 17

Chapter 4 Reframing Your Mindset 23

Chapter 5 Building a Positive Lifestyle 29

Chapter 6 Positivity in Action 44

Conclusion: 58

Reflection Exercises......................................82

A note from the Author 85

The Power of Positive Thinking

Introduction:

The world we live in presents many challenges with a great deal of uncertainty and constant change. The power of positive thinking stands as a shining example, offering hope, resilience and direction.

Positive thinking is more than just wishful optimism - it is a mindset, a conscious decision to focus on solutions, opportunities and personal growth.

Unlike unrealistic or naive optimism, which ignores challenges or denies reality, a positive mindset acknowledges difficulties while choosing to approach them with hope, strength and a focus on actionable solutions. By embracing positivity, you will empower yourself to approach life with a sense of purpose, confidence and clarity.

A clear example of this is a motto used by a leading academy trust in the UK and they use three simple words: **Believe, Succeed, Achieve**

A positive attitude from day one for their students.

At its core, positive thinking shapes the way you view and respond to the world and influences your thoughts, emotions, behaviour and even your physical health.

By choosing positive thoughts, you create a ripple effect that enhances your personal well-being, strengthens your relationships and inspires those around you.

It is perhaps worth considering how you currently deal with a challenging situation and asking yourself whether or not it could have been dealt with better. Always be honest with yourself.

Similarly, a small act of kindness, such as offering encouragement or a smile to a friend, can lift their mood, which they may then pass on to others. Positivity spreads like ripples in a pond, starting with you at the centre and radiating outward to create a more uplifting and supportive environment for everyone.

In the course of this short book, you will without doubt note some degree of repetition, in particular affirmations. This is by design to remind you of what is required of you to achieve your goal.

This book is designed to help you explore how the practice of positive thinking can lead to a life of greater joy, resilience and success

A note from the author

In my own life, I have had many challenges and experienced a poor childhood, violence, fear, success, failure, grief, optimism, pessimism, highs and lows. It is how I dealt with these challenges that shaped my life.

A humble beginning; lack of confidence, achieving little at school, leaving at 15 to a life of 'job hopping' within very different industries. What I didn't realise was that all these lessons were preparing me for the life I have today.

So, what was it that changed or moulded me? Strict parents with little or no emotion left a mark on my life, which I didn't appreciate until I got older; what I did learn was that I should take responsibility for my actions.

Having married young, like most young men, we were taught that we had to 'put food on the table' and that meant working longer hours and sometimes two jobs at a time, it was a good work ethic and one which we never questioned.

During those years of working either as a barman, a school caretaker or a salesman, one small success gave me so much inspiration; I helped a business grow, the business owner was grateful and I was inspired and this gave me some foundation for my future career, in whatever direction that was going to be.

I soon realised that if you help another person or business, in my case, the rewards come back during your life, and it makes you understand that by being positive with and helping other people, you create happiness in their lives as well as your own.

These were important lessons that, at that time I did not really understand, but today I see the real value of those positive acts and probably the reason why I have achieved happiness in my own life.

I didn't have a name for it, I couldn't identify it and there were no written publications. Later in life I came to understand that it was my own positivity that helped create the life I have today.

I want to share these experiences with you to help you to believe in your own capabilities. This book is not intended to be 'mind-blowing.' On the contrary, it is deliberately concise and pocket-sized, to be used, sometimes as a short reminder.

It doesn't matter what your lifestyle is or what kind of job you do. Thinking in a positive manner is, without doubt, better for your health.

We are all human, and there are times when we need help or encouragement, please read on....

Inspirational Quotations:

> "Weed out self-doubt and sow confidence in its place."
> *Kevin Gould*

"Success is not final, failure is not fatal: it is the courage to continue that counts."
Winston Churchill

> "Happiness is not something ready-made. It comes from your own actions."
> Dalai Lama

"No one is useless in this world who lightens the burdens of another."
Charles Dickens

> "Hardships often prepare ordinary people for an extraordinary destiny."
> C S Lewis

Your thoughts are the roots of your reality - nurture them with care.
Kevin Gould

The Real Benefits of Positive Thinking

Why This Book Matters

This book provides you with the techniques, strategies and insights to unlock the full potential of positive thinking.

You will learn how to:

- Shift your mindset from negative to positive.
- Overcome limiting beliefs and develop empowering positive thought patterns.
- Cultivate gratitude, mindfulness and resilience.
- Build a positive lifestyle with actionable habits and achievable goals.
- Inspire and uplift others by spreading positivity in your community.

Positive thinking is not about ignoring reality or dismissing challenges; it is about choosing to focus on solutions, learning from experiences and believing in your ability to overcome.

Positivity coexists with realism; it acknowledges hardships and obstacles while maintaining hope and determination to rise above them. It is not blind optimism but an intentional effort to focus on what you can control, respond with resilience and build a constructive path forward.

As you journey through this short book, you will discover that positivity is not a destination but a lifelong practice, one that has the power to transform your mindset, your relationships and your life.

The diagram below illustrates the shift from a negative to a positive mindset, designed for a motivational and self-help context

The Benefits of Positive Thinking

IMPROVED HEALTH

BETTER RELATIONSHIPS

INCREASED RESILIENCE

GREATER HAPPINESS

ENHANCED PRODUCTIVIT

Chapter 1
Understanding the Mind

Understanding the Mind in Simple Terms: Think of the mind as a garden and your thoughts are the seeds.

Positive thoughts grow into beautiful, healthy plants, while negative thoughts can sprout weeds.

Just like a gardener tends to their garden, you can nurture positive thoughts to create a flourishing, healthy mindset.

The mind is powerful and what you focus on grows.

The Power of Thoughts: Our thoughts are the foundation of our reality; what we think shapes our beliefs, decisions and actions, which in turn create the world we experience.

For example, if you constantly think you will fail, you may avoid opportunities, hesitate to take risks or approach challenges with low energy, ultimately creating a reality where success feels out of reach.

On the other hand, positive thoughts build confidence and inspire action. When you believe in your abilities, you are more likely to take decisive steps, see opportunities and persist through challenges.

Thoughts act as a filter and influence how we perceive situations and the people around us. By choosing to focus on empowering constructive thoughts, you can reshape your reality for the better.

Optimism v Pessimism: Optimism and pessimism are two opposing lenses through which we view the world.

Optimism is the belief that things will improve or that good outcomes are possible, even in challenging situations. Optimists tend to focus on solutions, see set-backs as temporary and believe in their ability to overcome challenges. This mindset fosters resilience, motivation and action.

Pessimism, on the other hand, is the belief that things are likely to go wrong or that negative outcomes are inevitable.

Pessimists tend to dwell on problems, see set-backs as permanent and feel powerless to change their circumstances. While pessimism can sometimes help identify risks, an overly negative mindset can lead to inaction, stress and missed opportunities.

By cultivating optimism, you empower yourself to take control, persist and find opportunities for growth even when faced with adversity.

Understanding the Mind in Simple Terms:

Think of the mind as that team of gardeners inside your head. These people process everything you experience and decide how you feel or act.

Positive thoughts act like cheerleaders, encouraging the workers to find solutions, stay motivated and keep you happy.

Negative thoughts, on the other hand, can act like complainers, slowing the team down and making everything feel harder.

You are the leader of this team and by choosing which thoughts to focus on, you decide how well the team performs; the more you encourage the positive workers, the stronger and more efficient they become.

This simple idea shows that by nurturing positive thoughts, you can guide your mind to work better, feel better and help you create a happier life.

Let's keep this simple…

Science Behind Positivity: The science of positivity is grounded in neuroscience and psychology.

When we think positively, our brain releases chemicals like dopamine, serotonin and endorphins—often called the 'happy hormones.' These chemicals enhance our mood, reduce stress and promote overall well-being. A dose of happiness.

Research shows that positivity strengthens neural pathways in the brain, making it easier to form optimistic thought patterns over time. The brain also has neuroplasticity, the ability to rewire and adapt based on our experiences and habits. This means that practicing positive thinking can reshape the brain to favour more constructive and empowering thoughts.

Additionally, studies in psychology reveal that people with a positive mindset are more likely to experience lower levels of anxiety, improved immune function and increased longevity.

The diagram below illustrates the science behind positivity, featuring concepts like neuroplasticity, happiness chemicals and their effects on emotional and physical health.

The Science Behind Positivity

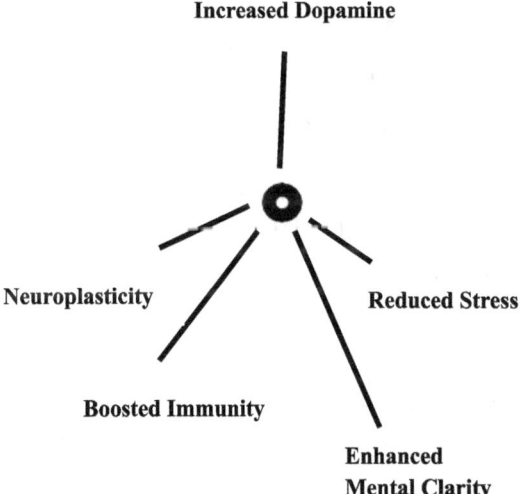

Chapter 2
Benefits of Positive Thinking

Below is a simple diagram illustrating the benefits of positive thinking, showcasing its impact on mental health, resilience, relationships and overall well-being.

> Improved physical health.
>
> Improved mental health.
>
> Increased physical well-being.
>
> Increased success.
>
> Reduced stress.
>
> Happiness.
>
> Greater resilience.
>
> Inner warmth.
>
> Self-confidence.

Health and Well-being: Positivity has a powerful impact on both your mental and physical health.

Mental Health: Positive thinking reduces your stress, anxiety and symptoms of depression.

When you focus on hopeful, empowering thoughts, your brain produces hormones, as already mentioned, like dopamine and serotonin, which naturally improve your mood and increase feelings of happiness. Over time, cultivating a positive mindset helps you develop emotional resilience, making it easier to manage life's challenges without becoming overwhelmed.

Physical Health: Research shows that a positive outlook will improve your physical health in remarkable ways; people who practice positivity often experience lower blood pressure, reduced inflammation and a stronger immune system.

Positivity also encourages us to consider healthy habits such as regular exercise, better sleep and proper nutrition, which all contribute to physical well-being. Studies even link a positive mindset to longer lifespans, showing that optimism can help you live a healthier, happier and longer life.

Resilience: Positive thinking plays a key role in building your resilience—and your own ability to bounce back from setbacks in life.

When faced with challenges, a positive mindset helps you see obstacles as opportunities for growth rather than insurmountable problems. Optimistic individuals are better equipped to reframe negative experiences, focus on solutions and persist through difficult and challenging times.

This resilience is not about ignoring pain or hardship but choosing to believe in the possibility of improvement. By nurturing positivity, you will create for yourself the emotional and mental strength to recover faster, learn from set-backs and keep moving forward toward your goals.

Success and Goal Achievement: Positive thinking has a direct link to success and achieving your goals; a positive mindset fuels motivation, persistence and clarity; key components needed to reach your dreams.

Optimistic individuals are more likely to set ambitious goals and take consistent actions toward achieving them because they believe success is possible. Positivity also allows you to view failures as learning experiences rather than final defeats, which encourages your own growth and improvement.

When you believe in yourself and your abilities, you will be better able to overcome obstacles, stay focused and turn aspirations into reality. In this way, positive thinking becomes the driving force that will help you unlock your full potential and succeed in life.

Relationships: A positive mindset will strengthen your connections by fostering kindness, understanding and open communication.

When you approach others with positivity, you will create an environment of trust and mutual respect. People are naturally drawn to those who uplift and inspire them, making it easier to form and maintain meaningful relationships. **Be that person.**

Positivity also helps you better handle conflicts, as an optimistic perspective allows you to see solutions rather than focus on blame or negativity. Additionally, a positive outlook will make you more empathetic, improving your ability to listen and understand other's emotions.

By maintaining a positive attitude, you will not only build stronger connections but also inspire those around you to embrace positivity as well.

Success!

Chapter 3
Identifying Negative Patterns:

- Self-doubt.
- Over thinking.
- Negative thoughts.
- Fear of failure.
- Not trusting those closest to you.
- Listening to negative people.
- Questioning your decisions—every decision.
- Saying to yourself "I'm not sure"
- Waiting too long to make any decision.
- Doubting your own ability.

Recognising Limiting Beliefs: Limiting beliefs are thoughts that will hold you back from reaching your full potential. They often sound like self-doubt, fear or negative assumptions.

To spot them:

Listen to Your Inner Dialogue: Pay attention to any recurring negative thoughts you may have. Examples include, "I'm not good enough," "I always fail" or "I don't deserve success."

Identify Patterns: Look for specific situations where these beliefs arise. Are they triggered by challenges, criticism or comparisons to others?

Past Experience: Because you might have failed with an action on a previous occasion, then failure is inevitable on anything new that you wish to do.

Question Their Validity: Ask yourself, "Is this thought true?" or, "What evidence do I have to support this belief?" Often, limiting beliefs are based on assumptions rather than facts.

Replace with Empowering Thoughts: Once you identify a limiting belief, replace it with a positive and empowering thought. For example, change "I can't do this," to "I will learn and improve step by step." Another example might be when you approach a challenging situation at work with calm and optimism, you will not only find solutions more effectively, but you will also influence your colleagues to remain hopeful and proactive.

Overcoming Negativity Bias: The brain has a natural tendency to focus more on negative experiences than positive ones. This is called negativity bias, and it served as a survival mechanism for our ancestors, helping them identify and avoid danger. However, in modern life, this bias can make us dwell on problems and overlook the good.

To overcome negativity bias:

Practice Gratitude: Actively write down three positive things that happened each day, no matter how small.

Reframe Experiences: When something negative happens, ask yourself, "What can I learn from this?" or "Is there a silver lining here?"

Celebrate Small Wins: Acknowledge and appreciate small achievements to shift focus away from perceived failures.

Mindful Awareness: Recognise when your mind is spiralling into negativity and gently redirect your focus toward solutions or neutral thoughts.

Self-Awareness: Techniques to assess your thought patterns.

Steps to Overcome Negative Bias

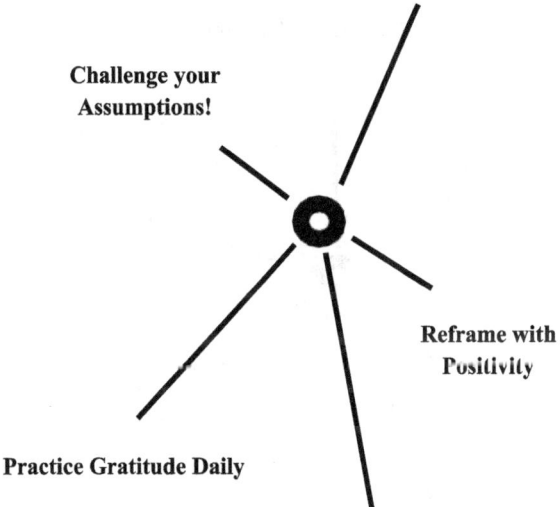

Recognise Negative Thoughts

Challenge your Assumptions!

Reframe with Positivity

Practice Gratitude Daily

Surround Yourself with Positivity

Below is a diagram illustrating the concept of self-awareness. It highlights key aspects like emotions, triggers and personal strengths to foster personal growth.

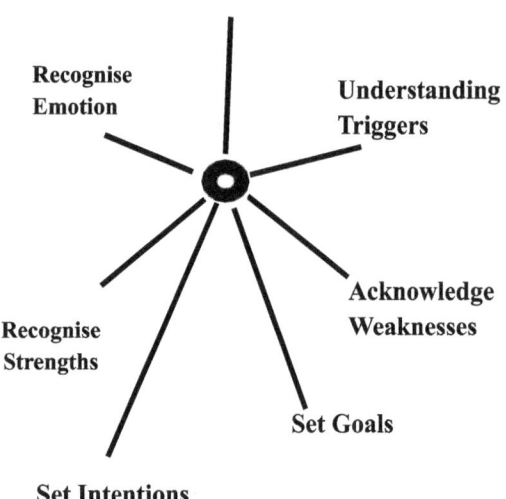

Make a Journal: Write down your thoughts and emotions on a regular basis, comfortable for you. Taking notes helps identify recurring patterns, triggers and areas of negativity.

Mindful Observation: Spend time observing your thoughts without judgment. Techniques like meditation or mindfulness can help you notice thought patterns as they arise.

Ask Reflective Questions: Use prompts such as:

"What thoughts hold me back the most?"
or
"Are my thoughts helping or hurting me?"

Thought-Tracking: Track your thoughts throughout the day by jotting them down or using apps designed for thought awareness.

Seek Feedback: Sometimes, friends or mentors can offer insights into the thought patterns they observe in you, providing valuable external perspectives.

Chapter 4
Reframing Your Mindset

Cognitive Reframing: Reframing your mindset begins with changing how you view and respond to negative thoughts. Cognitive reframing involves consciously challenging and replacing unhelpful thoughts with more positive or constructive ones.

Steps include:

- **Identify the Thought**: When you experience a negative thought, pause and write it down. For example: "I'm terrible at this task."

- **Challenge the Thought**: Ask yourself if the thought is accurate, fair or helpful. What evidence supports or contradicts it?

- **Replace the Thought**: Reframe it in a positive or neutral way. For example, replace "I'm terrible at this task." with "This is challenging, but I can learn and improve with effort."

- **Practice Regularly**: Reframing takes practice. Use this technique daily to build the habit of transforming negative thoughts into empowering ones.

The Power of Gratitude: Gratitude is the practice of focusing on and appreciating the positive aspects of your life, no matter how small.

When you embrace gratitude, you shift your attention away from what is lacking and toward what you already have. This shift in focus helps reduce your stress, improve your mood and foster a sense of contentment.

To harness the power of gratitude:

Keep a Journal: Write down three things you are grateful for each day. This simple habit can rewire your brain to focus on the positive.

Express Appreciation: Take time to thank people around you. A heartfelt thank-you strengthens relationships and spreads positivity.

Reflect on Challenges: Find something to be grateful for in difficult situations. Ask yourself, "What lesson can I learn from this?"

- **Savour Small Moments:** Take notice of small joys in your life; a beautiful sunset, a kind word or a quiet moment of peace.

- **Practice Gratitude Meditation:** Spend a few minutes each day meditating on things you are thankful for, visualising them and feeling that appreciation deeply.

Challenge the Thought: Ask yourself if the thought is true, helpful or based on facts. Consider what evidence supports or contradicts it.

Replace the Thought: Reframe the thought with a positive or neutral alternative. For example, replace "I'm not good at this" with "I'm learning and I will improve with practice."

Reinforce the Reframe: Repeat the new thought to yourself regularly to strengthen the positive perspective.

Shifting Your Thinking with Affirmations: Affirmations are short positive statements that help you reprogram your mindset and build confidence. They work by replacing negative self-talk with empowering beliefs, promoting optimism and motivation. Here is how to use affirmations effectively:

- **Identify Your Negative Thoughts**. Notice the specific thoughts that you hold back, such as "I can't do this" or "I'm not worthy."

- **Create Positive Affirmations**: Turn those thoughts into positive statements. Make affirmations personal, present tense and specific negative thoughts "I will always fail."

    Affirmation: "I am capable and I will

learn from my experience."

- **Repeat Daily**: Repeat your affirmations consistently, especially in the morning, before bed or during moments of doubt. Say them out loud, write them down or visualise them.

- **Feel the Words**: Connect emotionally to the affirmations. Imagine how it feels when they are true and focus on that feeling.

- **Be Consistent**: Affirmations are most effective when practiced regularly. Over time, they can reshape your thinking patterns and strengthen your confidence.

- **Use Visual Reminders**: Write your affirmations on sticky notes, place them where you will see them often (like a mirror or desk), or use affirmation apps.

Examples of Affirmations:

"I am strong, resilient and capable of overcoming challenges."

"I believe in myself and my ability to succeed."

"Every day, I grow more confident and positive."

"I am worthy of love, success and happiness."

Affirmations help you focus on what you want to believe and achieve. By repeating them, you create a mental shift, replacing limiting thoughts with empowering ones that support your goals and well-being.

Inspirational Quotations:

"Our greatest glory is not in never falling, but in rising every time we fall."

"You don't have to be great to start, but you have to start to be great."– Zig Ziglar

"You are the sum total of everything you've ever seen, heard, eaten, smelled, been told, forgot—it's all there." – Maya

"What lies behind us and what lies before us are tiny matters compared to what lies within us."

– Ralph Waldo Emerson

Chapter 5
Building a Positive Lifestyle

An illustration representing, "Building a Positive Life Style," symbolising growth, wellbeing and fulfilment.

Building a positive lifestyle means incorporating habits and routines that reinforce optimism, wellbeing and purpose. By making small but consistent changes, you can create an environment that supports your mindset and helps you thrive. Here are actionable steps to build a positive lifestyle:

Gratitude Practice

Gratitude helps shift your focus from what is lacking to what is abundant in your life.

- **Morning Gratitude**: Start your day by writing down three things for which you are grateful. These can be as simple as, "A good night's sleep," or "The support of a friend."

- **A 'Gratitude' Journal**: Maintain a daily journal where you reflect on moments, people or experiences that brought joy or value to your day.

- **Express Thanks**: Make it a habit to thank someone each day, whether it is a co-worker, friend or family member.

Mindfulness Practice

Mindfulness involves being fully present in the moment, helping to reduce stress and enhance clarity.

- **Meditation**: Spend 5-10 minutes each morning focusing on your breath or using a guided meditation app. There are plenty of them.

- **Mindful Activities**: Engage in everyday tasks like eating, walking or cleaning with full attention, appreciating the experience without distractions.

* **Body Scan**: Take a few moments to mentally scan your body, releasing tension and becoming aware of how you feel physically and emotionally.

Self-Care Routine

Taking care of yourself is essential for maintaining a positive outlook and energy levels.

* **Physical Activity**: Incorporate exercise into your day, whether it is yoga, walking or a gym workout. Movement releases endorphins, which boost mood.

* **Healthy Nutrition**: Fuel your body with nourishing foods that provide sustained energy and support mental clarity.

* **Adequate Sleep**: Aim for 7-8 hours of quality sleep each night to recharge your mind and body.

Positive Affirmations

Affirmations help reprogramme your mind by reinforcing empowering beliefs.

- **Morning Affirmations**: Begin your day with positive affirmations such as, "I have set and will do my utmost to achieve my goals today.

- **Visual Cues**: Keep a note of your affirmations so that you can refer to them and remind yourself of your goals for the day.

- **Reflection Time**: Take a few moments to identify how these affirmations are working that day.

Connection and Kindness

Positivity is amplified when shared with others.

- Acts of Kindness: Perform small acts of kindness daily, such as complimenting someone or lending a helping hand.

- **Meaningful Conversations**: Spend time connecting deeply with a friend, family member or colleague.

- **Digital Detox**: Set boundaries for screen time and prioritise face-to-face interactions to strengthen relationships.

Reflection and Recording

Recording allows you to process emotions, track progress and clarify your thoughts.

- **Daily Reflection**: Write about one positive experience you had during the day.

- **Tracking Progress**: Note any shifts in your mindset or accomplishments toward your goals.

- **Question Prompts**: Use prompts like "What made me smile today?" or, "What lesson did I learn today?"

Celebrate Small Wins

Recognising your efforts and achievements, no matter how small, reinforces a positive mindset.

- **Daily Rewards**: Treat yourself to something enjoyable when you complete a task or overcome a challenge.

- **Victory List**: Keep a list of your daily wins to remind yourself of your progress.

- **End-of-Day Gratitude**: Reflect on the day's successes, no matter how minor they may seem.

By integrating these habits into your daily routine, you can create a strong foundation for positivity, resilience and personal growth. The key is consistency, small actions repeated over time lead to transformative change.

Daily Habits for Cultivating Positivity

Building positivity into your daily routine creates a foundation for lasting change. By practicing simple intentional habits, you can nurture a positive mindset and improve your overall well-being.

Here are some daily habits to incorporate into your life:

The following diagram illustrates daily habits for cultivating positivity. Each segment highlights key practices like gratitude, mindfulness, acts of kindness and more.

The Impact of Relationships on Positivity

* Supportive Connections: Build relationships with people who uplift and encourage you. Supportive friends and family members can help you see the bright side of situations and motivate you to stay positive.

* Limit Toxic Influences: Minimise interactions with people who drain your energy or consistently focus on negativity; protecting your mental well-being is essential for sustaining positivity.

* Engage in Meaningful Interactions: Prioritise quality over quantity in your relationships. Deep and meaningful conversations strengthen bonds and promote mutual growth.

* Practice Active Listening: Show genuine interest in others by listening attentively and responding empathetically. This creates an environment of trust and positivity.

* Join Positive Groups: Participate in communities or clubs that align with your values and interests. These groups often foster encouragement

and shared growth.

- Volunteer: Helping others creates a sense of purpose and spreads positivity both to those you help and within yourself.

- Celebrate Together: Share successes and milestones with your community to amplify joy and build stronger connections.

Digital Environment

- Curate Your Online Presence: Follow accounts and engage with content that inspires, educates or uplifts you. Don't follow sources of negativity or stress.

- Practice Mindful Technology Use: Set boundaries for screen time and take breaks from digital devices to maintain focus and reduce anxiety.

- Spread Positivity Online: Share uplifting messages, gratitude or helpful resources with your network to contribute to a positive digital environment.

* By cultivating a supportive environment and nurturing healthy relationships, you create a foundation that reinforces your positive mindset. Surrounding yourself with positivity

in both physical spaces and social interactions empowers you to stay resilient and optimistic in life's difficulties

The Power and Purpose of Setting Meaningful Goals

Goals are more than mere aspirations; they provide a roadmap for personal growth and fulfilment.

Setting meaningful goals aligns your actions with your values, gives you direction and fuels your motivation.

Here's how to harness the power of goal setting and ensure your goals serve a higher purpose:

Why Goals Matter

- Clarity of Vision: Goals give you a clear sense of what you want to achieve, making it easier to focus your energy and resources.

- Motivation and Momentum: When you set achievable milestones, you create a sense of accomplishment that propels you forward.

- Purposeful Living: Goals grounded in your values and passions give meaning to your efforts and ensure that your actions align with your authentic self.

- Resilience in Challenges: A strong sense of purpose helps you navigate setbacks, adapt to change and stay committed to your journey.

Steps to Set Meaningful Goals

Reflect on Your Values:

- Identify what matters most to you - family, career, health, creativity or contribution to others.
- Ensure your goals align with these core values to maintain intrinsic motivation.

Make Goals SMART:

- Specific: Clearly define what you want to achieve.
- Measurable: Determine how you will track progress.
- Achievable: Set goals that challenge you but are within reach.
- Relevant: Align your goals with your values and priorities.
- Time-bound: Set deadlines to maintain focus and urgency.

1. Break Goals into Milestones:

- Divide larger goals into smaller, actionable steps to avoid feeling overwhelmed.
- Celebrate each milestone to build momentum and maintain positivity.

2. Visualise Success:

- Imagine achieving your goals and the positive impact they will have on your life.
- Use visualisation to stay motivated and focused during challenging times.

3. Stay Flexible

- Life is unpredictable; be willing to adapt your goals as circumstances change.
- Regularly review and adjust your goals to ensure they remain relevant.

4. Examples of Meaningful Goals

- **Personal Growth**: "Learn a new language in a year, perhaps longer, by practicing 15—20 minutes daily."
- **Health and Wellness**: "Run a 5K in six months by following a weekly training plan."
- **Career Advancement**: "Earn a professional qualification/certification within a year to enhance my skills."
- **Relationships**: "Spend one evening per week connecting with family without distractions."
- **Community Contribution**: "Volunteer at a local shelter twice a month to give back to my community."

5. The Power of Purpose-Driven Goals

Goals with a deeper purpose create lasting fulfilment:

- **Inspire Growth**: Goals push you to expand your comfort zone and discover new strengths.

"The future belongs to those who believe in the beauty of their dreams." – Eleanor Roosevelt

> "Act as if what you do makes a difference. It does."
>
> – William James

"Your mind is a powerful thing. When you fill it with positive thoughts, your life will start to change."

- Kevin Gould

Chapter 6
Positivity in Action

- Express Gratitude
- Encourage Others
- Smile More Often
- Engage in Acts of Kindness
- Practice Self Care

This section provides a deeper insight into how you can implement positivity in tangible ways.

1. Transforming Obstacles into Opportunities

Positivity allows you to see challenges as chances to grow rather than setbacks.

- **Example**: If a project at work does not go as planned, focus on what you can learn from the experience and how you can improve in the future.
- **Action Step**: Write down one lesson from a current difficulty and how it can benefit you moving forward.

2. Small, Consistent Actions for Big Change

Positivity in action thrives on daily habits that reinforce optimism.

- **Example**: Setting a goal to spend five minutes each morning visualising success and planning one proactive step for the day.
- **Action Step**: Commit to one positive action each day, whether it is recording, exercising, or offering help to someone.

3. Kindness as a 'Ripple Effect'

Kindness has a powerful 'ripple effect' that spreads positivity far beyond the act.

Example: Paying for a stranger's coffee or leaving a kind note for a colleague can brighten someone's day and inspire them to pay it forward. In this context, **"pay it forward"** means performing an act of kindness for someone else in response to the kindness you have received rather than repaying the person who was kind to you directly. The idea is to create a chain of goodwill where kindness spreads from one person to another, creating a positive ripple effect.

Example in Context

- If someone buys coffee for a stranger, the recipient might feel inspired to do something kind for someone else, like helping a neighbour or donating to a worthy cause.

- This concept encourages selflessness and the idea that kindness can grow and impact many lives beyond the initial act.

- **Action Step:**

Make a list of simple acts of kindness you can perform each week.

- Compliment someone

- Leave a kind note
- Help a neighbour.
- Donate an item.
- Pay for someone.
- Check in on a friend.
- Support a local business.
- Volunteer your time.
- Share something uplifting.
- Practice active listening.

Staying Solution - Oriented in Conflict

Positivity helps you focus on solutions rather than dwelling on problems.

- Example: In a disagreement, instead of blaming, work collaboratively to find common ground
- Action Step: Practice Framing your concerns as questions, such as "How can we address this together?"

4. Leading with Optimism

Being a role model of positivity can inspire others to adopt a similar mindset.

- **Example**: Staying calm and hopeful during a stressful situation can motivate your team to approach challenges with the same attitude.

- **Action Step**: Reflect on moments where you can intentionally lead by example in your daily life.

5. Building Deeper Connections Through Positivity

Empathy and encouragement strengthen relationships and foster mutual support.

- **Example**: Sending a friend a thoughtful message or actively listening during a conversation builds trust and connection.
- **Action Step**: Schedule a weekly check-in with a friend or loved one to nurture your bond.

Recognising and Celebrating Progress

Celebrating even small wins reinforces positivity and builds momentum.

- **Example**: Completing a task, meeting a fitness milestone or navigating a tough day successfully are all worthy of recognition.
- **Action Step**: Keep a "Progress Journal" to record and celebrate your achievements daily or weekly.

Visualising Positivity in Action
(please look at the diagram again)

Positivity in Action

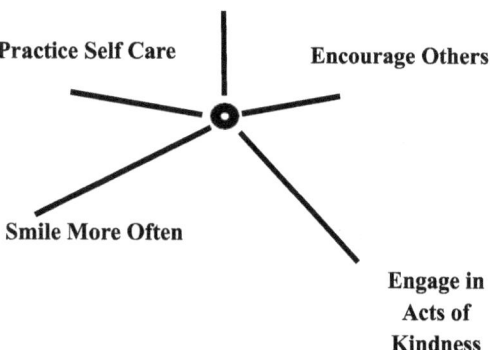

Applying Positivity in Real-Life Solutions

1. **Workplace Challenges**

    - **Scenario:** You're assigned a complex project with a tight deadline and initial attempts are not going as planned

    - **Positivity in Action**. Instead of succumbing to frustration, break the project into smaller manageable steps. Acknowledge your progress, no matter how small and seek support or collaborate with colleagues. Reframe the challenge as an opportunity to showcase both creativity and resilience.

    - **Result**: The project is completed with a new sense of accomplishment and your problem-solving skills are recognised

2. **Conflict in Relationships**

    - **Scenario**: A disagreement arises with a close friend over a misunderstanding.

    - **Positivity in Action**: Approach the conversation with empathy and a solution-oriented mindset. Actively listen to their perspective and express your feelings calmly. Use affirming statements like "I value our friendship and want to find a way forward."

- **Result**: The conflict is resolved and your bond is strengthened through mutual understanding and respect.

3. **Personal Set-backs**

    - **Scenario**: You did not achieve the results you hoped for in an important exam or interview.

    - **Positivity in Action**: Instead of dwelling on failure, reflect on the experience to identify areas for improvement. Develop a study or preparation plan for the next attempt and remind yourself of past successes to build confidence.

    - **Result**: You approach the next opportunity with greater preparation and resilience, improving your chances of success.

4. **Parenting or Mentoring**

    - **Scenario**: A child or mentee is feeling discouraged after struggling with a task or skill.

    - **Positivity in Action**: Share words of encouragement, focusing on their efforts rather than the outcome. Help them reframe mistakes as learning opportunities and set small, achievable goals to build their confidence.

- **Result**: They develop a growth mindset and become more willing to face challenges.

5. **Health & Wellbeing**

    - **Scenario**: You're trying to adopt a healthier lifestyle but find it difficult to stay consistent with exercise or nutrition goals.

    - **Positivity in Action**: Celebrate small milestones, such as completing a short workout or making one healthy meal choice. Replace self-criticism with affirmations like, "I'm making progress, one step at a time."

    - **Result**: You sustain long-term habits and achieve your health goals without overwhelming yourself.

6. **Community Engagement**

    - **Scenario**: You notice a need for improvement in your local community, such as littering or lack of social programs.

- **Positivity in Action**: Organise a clean-up event or volunteer your time to start a positive initiative. Invite friends and neighbours to join, creating a ripple effect of goodwill.
- **Result**: The community benefits from your efforts, and others are inspired to take positive action.

7. **Organising Community Projects**

    - **Example**: Start a community garden, organise a neighbourhood clean-up or create a book club.
    - **Impact**: Builds a sense of connection and shared purpose among participants.

8. **Financial Challenges**

    - **Scenario**: You face unexpected expenses that strain your budget.
    - **Positivity in Action**: Instead of panicking, create a plan to address the situation. List practical steps, such as cutting discretionary spending or seeking additional income opportunities. Focus on gratitude for what you can manage and the support you have.
    - **Result**: You regain control over your

finances and learn valuable budgeting skills for the future.

Each of these examples illustrates how positivity isn't just an abstract concept but a practical tool to approach and resolve real-life challenges. By cultivating optimism, you can turn obstacles into opportunities, build stronger relationships and foster personal and professional growth.

The Role of Environment and Relationships in Sustaining Positivity

Your environment and relationships play a crucial role in fostering and sustaining a positive mindset. Surrounding yourself with uplifting spaces and supportive people can significantly impact your outlook on life and your ability to maintain positivity.

Creating a Positive Physical Environment

- **Declutter Your Space:** A clean and organised space promotes clarity and reduces stress. Start by decluttering your home, workspace, or any area where you spend considerable time.

- **Incorporate Nature:** Bring elements of nature indoors, such as plants, flowers or natural light, to create a calming and uplifting atmosphere.

- **Personalise Your Space:** Surround yourself with items that bring you joy, like photos, artwork or inspiring quotes.

- **Choose Colours Wisely:** Use colours that evoke positivity and calmness, such as blue, green or yellow in your decor.

Spreading positivity to others and creating a supportive community

Spreading positivity extends beyond individual efforts. It involves uplifting others and fostering an environment where positivity thrives. Here are practical examples:

1. **Acts of Kindness**

    - **Example**: Volunteer at a local shelter, donate to a cause or help a neighbour with their groceries.

    - **Impact**: These small, thoughtful gestures create a chain reaction of kindness, inspiring others to give back.

2. **Sharing Positive Stories**

    - **Example**: Share uplifting news or personal success stories with friends, family or on social media.

    Impact: Positivity becomes contagious, encouraging others to see the good around them.

3. **Creating a Safe Space**

    Example: Host regular meet-ups where friends or colleagues can share challenges and achievements without fear of judgment.

    - **Impact**: Fosters trust, openness and mutual support within the group.

4. **Encouraging Growth**

    - **Example**: Offer to mentor someone in your field or encourage a friend to pursue a personal goal.

    - **Impact**: Empowering others builds confidence and inspires further action.

5. **Celebrating Others**

    - **Example**: Recognise and celebrate achievements, whether it's a promotion, a personal milestone, or overcoming a challenge.

    - **Impact**: Reinforces a culture of encouragement and mutual respect.

6. **Supporting Mental Wellness**

    - **Example**: Encourage someone struggling with stress or anxiety to seek help and offer a listening ear.
    - **Impact**: Promotes resilience and emotional well-being in your community.

Spreading positivity and creating a supportive community fosters a ripple effect that transforms not only individual lives but also the collective atmosphere. By taking small, intentional steps, you can be a catalyst for lasting change.

Conclusion:

Recap of Key Insights

Throughout this journey into positive thinking, we have explored actionable strategies, habits and examples to transform your mindset and life.

Here is a summary of the key takeaways:

1. **Positivity Begins with Awareness**

    - Recognise your thought patterns and identify areas where negativity is holding you back.
    - Use tools like journaling, mindfulness and self-reflection to understand your mental habits.

2. **Daily Habits Build Momentum**

    - Simple practices such as gratitude recording, mindfulness and affirmations create a foundation for lasting positivity.
    - Consistency is key—small daily actions lead to transformative change over time.

3. **Positivity in Action Creates Ripple Effects**

    - Applying positivity in real-life scenarios, such as resolving conflicts, setting goals or supporting others, enhances both personal and communal growth.

    - Acts of kindness and solution-focused thinking foster an environment where positivity thrives.

4. **Community and Relationships Matter**

    - Building a supportive network amplifies positivity. Celebrate, encourage and uplift those around you.

    - A positive environment, both physical and social, reinforces your mindset and inspires others.

5. **Challenges Are Opportunities**

    - Obstacles are stepping stones for growth. Reframe setbacks as learning experiences and approach them with a solution-oriented mindset.

    - Resilience is built through practice and perspective.

6. Spread Positivity Beyond Yourself

- Be a beacon of positivity by leading with optimism and sharing your growth with others.

- Inspire and engage in community efforts to create a ripple effect of positive change.

By embracing these principles, you can create a life filled with purpose, joy and resilience while inspiring those around you to do the same. Positivity is a lifelong journey - one that begins with small, intentional steps but leads to profound transformations.

Don't forget

Look for the opportunity in the problem and not the problem in the opportunity.

Kevin Gould

Encouragement to Make Positivity a Lifelong Practice

Positivity is not a one-time effort or a quick fix, it is a continuous practice that grows and evolves with you. Here's why and how you can make positivity a lifelong commitment:

1. A Foundation for Resilience

Life is full of challenges, but a positive mindset helps you bounce back stronger each time. By consistently practicing positivity, you equip yourself with the tools to navigate adversity with hope and determination.

2. The Compound Effect of Small Actions

Small positive habits, when practiced daily, lead to significant changes over time. Just as compound interest grows wealth, consistent positivity builds emotional resilience, mental clarity and personal fulfilment.

3. Creating a Legacy of Positivity

Your actions influence those around you. By embodying positivity, you inspire others to adopt similar practices, creating a ripple effect that can transform lives, workplaces and communities.

4. Growth Through Reflection and Adaptation

A lifelong practice of positivity encourages continual growth. Regular reflection helps you adapt your mindset to new challenges and opportunities, ensuring that you remain aligned with your goals and values.

5. A Life of Fulfilment and Joy

Positivity enhances your overall quality of life. By focusing on gratitude, celebrating progress and spreading kindness, you cultivate a sense of contentment and purpose that enriches every aspect of your journey.

"The only place where your dream becomes impossible is in your own thinking." – Robert H. Schuller

"When you have a positive mindset, you can't be defeated." – Joel Osteen

Practical Steps to Sustain Positivity

1. **Commit to Daily Practices**: Schedule time each day for gratitude, mindfulness and affirmations.

2. **Reflect Regularly**: Review your progress and adapt your habits as needed.

3. **Surround Yourself with Positivity**: Build relationships and environments that nurture optimism.

4. **Inspire Others**: Share your journey and encourage others to embrace positivity.

5. **Celebrate Growth**: Acknowledge how far you've come and look forward to continued progress.

By making positivity a lifelong practice, you not only transform your own life but also contribute to a more uplifting and hopeful world. The journey is ongoing, but every step brings you closer to a life of joy, purpose and resilience.

Call to Action: Choose Positivity Every Day

The journey of positivity is an ongoing commitment, one that transforms not only your life but also the lives of those around you. Making positivity a daily practice begins with small, intentional actions that create lasting change.

Don't put off to tomorrow, what can be done today.

Weekly Action Plan

Daily Practice for gratitude, mindfulness and affirmation.

Just tick each day √ for each achievement

Gratitude:

Sun	Mon	Tue	Wed	Thu	Sa

Mindfulness

Sun	Mon	Tue	Wed	Thu	Sa

Affirmations:

Sun	Mon	Tue	Wed	Thu	Sa

By choosing positivity every day, you will empower yourself to live with intention, resilience and purpose. This daily practice not only transforms your own life but also inspires others to adopt positivity, creating a ripple effect that extends far beyond yourself.

30-Day Positivity Challenge: An Action Plan

This 30-day challenge is designed to help you build a sustainable positivity practice through small, actionable steps. Each day focuses on a specific activity that reinforces positive thinking, mindfulness and connection.

> Inspirational quotation:
> Your mind is a garden.
> Your thoughts are the seeds.
> You can grow flowers
> or
> you can grow weeds.

Week 1: Gratitude and Awareness

Actions

- **Day 1 (Sunday)**: Write down three things you are grateful for.

    Task Fulfilled? **Note what they are.**

- **Day 2 (Monday)**: Identify one negative thought and reframe it positively.

    Task Fulfilled? **Write it down.**

- **Day 3 (Tuesday)**: Send a message of appreciation to someone who has positively impacted your life.

    Task Fulfilled? Record it.

- **Day 4 (Wednesday)**: Spend 5 minutes observing your thoughts without judgment.

    Task Fulfilled? Write it down.

- **Day 5 (Thursday)**: Start a gratitude journal and commit to writing in it daily.

    Task Fulfilled? Start that journal.

- **Day 6 (Friday)**: Share something you're thankful for with a friend or colleague.

    Task Fulfilled? Share it.

- **Day 7 (Saturday)**: Reflect on the week and write about one positive experience you had.

    - **Task Fulfilled**? Reflect on the week and 'pat your back'

Week 2: Building Positive Habits

Actions

- **Day 8 (Sunday)**: Begin your day with a positive affirmation.

  Task Fulfilled? Write it down.

- **Day 9 (Monday)**: Take a 10-minute walk outdoors and focus on the beauty around you.

  Task Fulfilled? Do it!

- **Day 10 (Tuesday)**: Perform one random act of kindness.

  Task Fulfilled? Feel good.

- **Day 11 (Wednesday)**: Declutter a small space in your home or workspace.

  Task Fulfilled? Yes

- **Day 12 (Thursday)**: Write about a challenge you overcame and what you learned.

  Task Fulfilled? Be proud!

- **Day 13 (Friday)**: Practice mindful breathing for 5 minutes.

  Task Fulfilled? Feel relaxed.

- **Day 14 (Saturday)**: Share a success story or inspiring thought with your social circle.
- **Task Fulfilled**? Feel proud!

Week 3: Deepening Connections

- **Day 15 (Sunday)**: Plan a meaningful conversation with someone you value.

    Task Fulfilled? Note the chat.

- **Day 16 (Monday)**: Compliment someone genuinely.

    Task Fulfilled? **Note who, mean it.**

- **Day 17 (Tuesday)**: Dedicate 30 minutes to a hobby or activity that brings you joy.

    Task Fulfilled? You deserve it!!

- **Day 18 (Wednesday)**: Reflect on how you can support someone in need and take action.

    Task Fulfilled? - Both feel good.

- **Day 19 (Thursday)**: Reconnect with an old friend through a call or message.

  Task Fulfilled? - Good to catch up. **Note it.**

- **Day 20 (Friday)**: Spend time volunteering or helping your community.

  Task Fulfilled? - **Make a note.**

- **Day 21 (Saturday)**: Record the relationships that bring positivity into your life.

  Task Fulfilled? - **Very Important!!**

Week 4: Sustaining Positivity

- **Day 22 (Sunday)**: Visualise a goal you want to achieve and write down actionable steps.

  Task Fulfilled? Note it.

- **Day 23 (Monday)**: Create a list of affirmations that resonate with your current goals.

  Task Fulfilled? - Note them.

- **Day 24 (Tuesday)**: Spend 15 minutes meditating on positive emotions.

    Task Fulfilled? - Important - do it!

- **Day 25 (Wednesday)**: Reflect on a set back and identify the lessons learned.

    Task Fulfilled? – Write it and honest.

- **Day 26 (Thursday)**: Write about how positivity has impacted your life so far.

    Task Fulfilled? - Uplifting note.

- **Day 27 (Friday)**: Share your positivity journey with a friend or group.

    Task Fulfilled? - Uplifting note.

Day 28 (Saturday): Write down three positive changes you want to maintain long term.

Task Fulfilled? - Note and keep them close.

1

2

3

Final Days: Reflection and Celebration

- **Day 29 (Sunday)**: Reflect on your 30-day journey. What has changed? What have you learned?

- **Day 30 (Monday)**: Celebrate your progress! Treat yourself to something meaningful and plan how you will continue your journey of positivity.

Recording/Journal Prompts and Reflection Exercises

Recording or making a journal is a powerful tool for self-awareness and cultivating positivity. Below are examples of prompts and exercises designed to help you reflect, grow and maintain a positive outlook.

Actions

Use this as a reminder of your journey and refer to it. Note the lessons gained and learn from them.

Well done!! You have now set your future course -time for a treat— go on, you deserve it!

Gratitude-Focused Prompts

- What are three things you are grateful for today and why?
- Describe a moment from this week that brought you joy or peace.
- Who has made a positive impact on your life recently, and how can you show appreciation?

Self-Awareness Prompts

- What are three qualities you admire about yourself?
- Identify one area of your life where you have grown in the past year. How did you achieve this growth?
- Write about a time when you turned a challenge into an opportunity.

Growth and Positivity Prompts

- What positive habits have helped you feel more grounded and happier?
- Describe a recent success. What actions did you take to achieve it?
- Write about a person or experience that inspires you to keep growing.

Notes:

Notes:

Reflection Exercises

1. **Daily Positivity Tracker:**

   - Write down one positive moment or thought each day.

   - At the end of the week, review your entries and identify patterns.

2. **Challenge Reflection:**

   - Reflect on a recent obstacle and write about how you overcame it.

   - Note the lessons you learned and how you can apply them in the future.

3. **Vision Mapping:**

   - Imagine your ideal life 5 years from now. Describe it in detail, focusing on emotions, relationships and accomplishments.

   - Identify one step you can take today to move closer to that vision.

4. **Kindness Log:**

   - Record daily acts of kindness you performed and how they made you feel.

   - Reflect on how these actions may have impacted others.

5. **Weekly Check-In:**

    - What went well this week and what could be improved?
    - How did you practice positivity and what were the results?
    - Set orientation for the upcoming week.

By incorporating these journal prompts and reflection exercises into your routine, you can deepen yourself.

Your journey starts here and remember

"Every day may not be good, but there's something good in every day."

– Alice Morse Earle

"Your mind is a powerful thing When you fill it with positive Thoughts, your life will start to change"

      Kazoo Ishiguro

    "The best way the cheer yourself is to try to cheer someone else up"

      Mark Twain

"Believe you can and you're halfway there"

    Theodore Roosevelt

    "Our greatest glory is not in never failing but in rising every time we fall"

      Confucius

  "Happiness depends on ourselves"

     Aristotle

Dear Reader

This book is designed to be a constant companion; it does not want to be sat on a bookshelf collecting dust and perhaps viewed 'once in a blue moon'.

It does not seek to delve too deeply into the mind, on the contrary, it is intended to give encouragement and self-belief DAILY.

It is deliberately pocket-sized so that it can be kept in your bag, your pocket, or on your desktop for employers to give to their employees to help create a successful working environment, for employees, for schools and colleges to give students inspiration.

The journey starts here and needs to continue—keep this book with you and use it to keep those positive thoughts or to encourage you when you perhaps feel that your confidence might have slipped.

Be proud to show to your friends, be proud of being positive, be proud of yourself!

Kevin M Gould

Notes:

Notes:

Notes:

Notes:

www.ingramcontent.com/pod-product-compliance
Lightning Source LLC
Chambersburg PA
CBHW071909070526
44583CB00016B/1909